40 Recipes to Celebrate National Grapefruit Month

Appetizers, Sides, Lite Bites, Mains and Desserts: Grapefruit, it's not just for Breakfast!

BY

Stephanie Sharp

Warning - Disclaimer

The purpose of this book is to educate and entertain. The author and does not guarantee that anyone following these techniques, suggestions, tips, ideas, or strategies will become successful. The author shall have neither liability nor responsibility to anyone with respect to any loss or damage caused, or alleged to be caused, directly or indirectly by the information contained in this book.

Thank you so much for purchasing my book! As a reward for your purchase, you can now receive free books sent to you every day. All you have to do is just subscribe to the list by entering your email address in the box below and I will send you a notification every time I have a free promotion running. The books will absolutely be free with no work at all from you!

Who doesn't want free books? No one! There are free and discounted books every day, and an email is sent to you 1-2 days beforehand to remind you so you don't miss out. It's that easy!

Just visit the link or scan QR-code to get started!

https://stephanie-sharp.subscribemenow.com

Table of Contents

Introduction

National Grapefruit Month is the perfect opportunity to enjoy this bitter-sweet citrus fruit.

To honor this fantastic fruit, discover our 12 fun facts and find out just why you should enjoy grapefruit 24/7.

- The grapefruit first arrived in Florida in 1823. It was brought by Count Odet Philippe
- In 1963 Count Odet Philippe was inducted into the Citrus Hall of Fame
- Grapefruit trees grow to a height of around 25-30 feet

- Just one grapefruit tree produces more than 1500 pounds of fruit
- The Texas Red Grapefruit is the official fruit of Texas
- Every February the nation celebrates National Grapefruit Month
- Grapefruit is cholesterol and sodium-free
- Just one half of grapefruit gives you approximately 60 percent of your daily requirement of Vitamin C
- The first grapefruit found growing in Barbados in 1789, was described by naturalist and Welsh author, Reverend Griffith Hughes, as the forbidden fruit
- Eating grapefruit may improve the body's insulin resistance. It is also believed to aid weight loss
- The grapefruit season runs October through May
- There are a little over 50 calories in one serving of grapefruit

So throughout February why not honor National Grapefruit Month by cooking and baking with this versatile fruit.

Appetizers, Lite Bites, and Sides

BBQ Pork Belly Sliders

Juicy pork belly sliders served with red cabbage, and homemade ginger grapefruit chutney is the perfect lite bite or appetizer.

Servings: 12

Total Time: 8hours 35mins

Ingredients:

Marinade:

- ½ cup freshly squeezed orange juice
- ¾ cup water
- ½ cup soy sauce
- ¼ cup shallot (minced)
- ¼ cup hoisin sauce
- 3 tbsp lemongrass (minced)
- 2 tbsp freshly squeezed lime juice
- 2 tbsp honey
- 2 tbsp sugar
- 1 tbsp Chinese 5-spice powder
- 1 tbsp garlic (minced)
- 1 tbsp ginger (minced)
- 1 tbsp fish sauce
- 1½ tsp orange zest
- 1 tsp sriracha sauce

Pork Belly:

- 3 pounds pork belly (skins removed)
- 12 slider buns (steamed)
- 2 cups red cabbage (shredded)
- Ginger Grapefruit Chutney:
- ½ cup sugar
- ½ cup rice vinegar
- 2 cups fresh grapefruit segments
- 1 tbsp ginger (minced)
- 1 tsp curry powder

Directions:

1. First, prepare the marinade. In a bowl, combine the orange juice, water, soy sauce, shallot, hoisin sauce, lemongrass, lime juice, honey, sugar, Chinese 5-spice powder, garlic, ginger, fish sauce, orange zest, and sriracha sauce and mix to combine.

2. Place the pork belly in a baking pan, pour the marinade over the pork, cover and transfer to the fridge, overnight.

3. To prepare the chutney. In a pan, combine the sugar with the vinegar and over moderate heat, simmer until the mixture reduces by half.

4. Add the segments of grapefruit followed by the ginger and curry powder and simmer until the liquid is evaporated. Remove from the heat and set to one side.

5. Remove the pork belly from the marinade and set aside.

6. Slice the pork into ¾ "thick slices and cut into lengths of 3".

7. Cook the pork belly on both sides until crisp and brown.

8. Add some of the marinade set aside earlier to the pan and glaze the pork.

9. While the pork browns, warm the slider buns in a steamer.

10. Serve the pork on the buns.

11. Top with red cabbage and a dollop of homemade chutney.

Eggs Benedict with Grapefruit Hollandaise

Breakfast, brunch or a lite-bite, it doesn't get much better than this recipe for Eggs Benedict.

Servings: 4

Total Time: 30mins

Ingredients:

Eggs Benedict:

- 4 slices bacon
- 1 tbsp vegetable oil
- 1 tbsp vinegar
- 4 medium eggs
- Grapefruit segments
- 2 English muffins (halved, toasted)
- Hollandaise Sauce:
- ½ cup butter
- 5 egg yolks
- ¼ cup freshly squeezed grapefruit juice
- 1 tsp grapefruit zest
- 1 tsp white wine vinegar
- Dash of cayenne
- Pinch of salt

Directions:

1. In a cast iron frying pan, over moderately high heat, cook the bacon in the oil for a couple of minutes on each side.

2. Add the vinegar to a small pot of water and bring to a gentle simmer.

3. Using a spoon, create a whirlpool in the water and carefully add one egg.

4. Cook for between 4-5 minutes, before removing with a slotted spoon.

5. Repeat the process with the remaining 3 eggs.

6. Next, make the sauce. In a pot, bring 1" of water to simmer. Place a metal mixing bowl on top to create a double boiler.

7. Add the butter to the bowl, and melt. Remove the bowl from the heat.

8. In a second bowl, whisk the egg yolks along with the grapefruit juice and zest, white wine vinegar and a dash of cayenne.

9. Transfer the yolk mixture to heat over the pot of water, whisking until thickened.

10. Gradually, drizzle the butter into the egg mixture, until incorporated.

11. Top each muffin halves with bacon, and a poached egg.

12. Drizzle hollandaise sauce over the top and serve with segments of grapefruit.

Grapefruit Bruschetta

A healthy take on regular bruschetta that is ideal for anyone who doesn't like cheese.

Servings: 6-8

Total Time: 15mins

Ingredients:

- 1 baguette (sliced on the bias)
- 2 large cloves garlic (peeled, halved)
- 3-4 ripe Roma tomatoes (seeded, chopped)
- 1 cup grapefruit sections (chopped)
- 1 large avocado (peeled, pitted, chopped)
- ½ small red onion (peeled, chopped)
- ¼ cup cilantro (chopped)
- Olive oil
- Salt and black pepper
- Grapefruit segments (to garnish)
- Sprigs of cilantro (to garnish)

Directions:

1. Preheat the main oven to 350 degrees F.

2. Arrange the slices of baguette on a cookie sheet and toast until golden, for 5-7 minutes.

3. Rub the toasted sides of the bread with the cut side of the garlic and set to one side.

4. In a bowl, combine the tomatoes with the grapefruit, avocado, red onion, cilantro, oil, and seasoning, and toss to combine gently.

5. Spoon the grapefruit mixture over the bruschetta and garnish with segments of grapefruit and sprigs of cilantro.

6. Serve.

Grapefruit Guacamole

Grapefruit helps to absorb the nutrients in the avocado, meaning that not only is the combination of fruits tasty but good for you too.

Servings: 4

Total Time: 7mins

Ingredients:

- 1 grapefruit
- 2 large avocados (peeled, pitted, mashed)
- 1 small onion (peeled, diced, rinsed)
- 1 jalapeno pepper (minced)
- ¼ cup fresh cilantro (chopped)
- ¼ tsp salt

Directions:

1. Cut the grapefruit in half, crosswise.

2. Over a bowl, to catch the juices and using a serrated spoon carefully scoop out the flesh from each pocket.

3. Add the avocado, onion, jalapeno pepper, and cilantro and mash with a fork.

4. Taste, season and serve.

Mixed Grapefruit with Ricotta, Cardamom, and Honey

The warmth of cardamom is in stark contrast to the bittersweet taste of grapefruit and sweet honey. Combine these flavors with creamy ricotta, and you have a first-class appetizer.

Servings: 4

Total Time: 25mins

Ingredients:

- 1 white grapefruit
- 1 pink grapefruit
- 1 ruby red grapefruit
- 6 whole green cardamom pods (lightly crushed)
- ½ cup honey
- 1⅓ cups fresh ricotta
- Ground black pepper

Directions:

1. First, supreme the grapefruits by trimming the top and bottom. Set cut-side facing upwards and lengthwise, slice between the flesh and the peel, following the shape of the fruit. Remove the peel along with the pith.

2. Over a bowl, slice between one segment and the membrane lengthwise until you reach the middle of the fruit.

3. Make a similar slice on the other side and using the knife blade, remove the segment. Repeat the process.

4. When all of the segments are successfully removed, squeeze the juice from the membrane into the mixing bowl.

5. Discard the membrane and set the juice aside for alternative use.

6. In a small pan, over moderate-high heat, toast the cardamom.

7. Add ¼ cup water followed by the honey, stirring to incorporate.

8. Bring to boil before reducing the heat to a simmer, and simmer for 5 minutes before allowing to cool.

9. Arrange the grapefruit over the fresh ricotta and drizzle with cardamom honey and season with pepper.

Nutty Grapefruit Quinoa

Top nutty quinoa with grapefruit and enjoy a flavor and texture-rich side dish.

Servings: 6-8

Total Time: 1hour 5mins

Ingredients:

- 3 tbsp olive oil
- 1 cup dry quinoa
- ½ cup almonds (sliced)
- ½ cup pine nuts
- 2 cups green onions (thinly sliced, divided)
- 1-1½ cups freshly squeezed grapefruit juice (divided)
- 1-1½ cups chicken stock (divided)
- ¼ tsp cayenne pepper
- Salt and black pepper
- 2 medium grapefruits (segmented, seeded, chopped)

Directions:

1. Over moderate heat, in a pan, heat the oil.

2. Add the quinoa and while stirring, cook until the quinoa begins to become golden brown, this will take approximately 5 minutes.

3. Stir in the almonds along with the pine nuts, and while stirring, cook for between 2-3 minutes, until the nuts are toasted.

4. Add 1½ cups of onions along with 1 cup freshly squeezed grapefruit juice, 1 cup of chicken stock, cayenne pepper, and seasoning, stirring to incorporate.

5. Bring to boil, before reducing the heat to a simmer, cover with a lid, and cook for 20 minutes while occasionally simmering.

6. Add the grapefruit juice plus the chicken stock, if necessary.

7. Remove from the heat, stir in the grapefruit along with the remaining green onions. Cover with a lid and allow to sit for 5 minutes.

8. Using a fork, fluff and serve.

Pasta Salad with Grapefruit, Blood Orange, and Kale

Not all salads have to be completely green, this refreshing fruity salad with grapefruit and orange is the perfect way to begin a meal.

Servings: 4

Total Time: 20mins

Ingredients:

- 8 ounces shell-shape pasta
- 1 large red grapefruit
- 1 large blood orange (seeded)
- ⅓ cup extra-virgin olive oil
- 1 tbsp grapefruit zest
- 2 tbsp orange juice
- 2 tbsp grapefruit juice
- 1 tbsp runny honey
- 1 cup kale (stems, removed, diced)
- ¼ red onion (peeled, thinly sliced)
- 2 tbsp red wine vinegar
- Salt and black pepper

Directions:

1. Cook the pasta according to the manufacturer's directions, until al dente. Drain and set aside to cool.

2. Zest the red grapefruit along with the blood orange.

3. Seed and slice both grapefruits into ¼" thick rounds and trim the rind.

4. Separate the fruit into chunks.

5. To prepare the dressing: In a small bowl, combine the oil with the zest, juices, and honey.

6. Add the pasta to a large mixing bowl.

7. Add the slices of grapefruit together with the orange, kale, onion and dressing and mix, to combine.

8. Taste and season.

9. Transfer to an airtight, resealable container until you are ready to serve.

10. Garnish with wedges of fruit.

Pink Grapefruit and Carrot Soup

A colorful and flavorsome soup to serve as an appetizer is always a welcome addition.

Servings: 4

Total Time: 35mins

Ingredients:

- 2 tsp butter
- ½ cup onion (peeled, minced)
- ½ cup pink grapefruit juice
- 3 cups chicken stock
- 1 cup carrot (diced)
- 1 cup potato (peeled, diced)
- Salt and black pepper
- Pinch of grated ginger
- ½ cup heavy cream
- ½ cup pink grapefruit (thinly sliced)

Directions:

1. In a pan over moderate heat, melt the butter.

2. Add the onion and cook until softened.

3. Using the grapefruit juice, deglaze the pan.

4. Pour in the chicken stock and add the carrots along with the potatoes.

5. Season with salt, black pepper and a pinch of grated ginger.

6. Bring to the boil and cook for between 20-25 minutes.

7. Transfer the soup to a blender and process until creamy.

8. Fold in the cream.

9. Garnish the soup with the slices of grapefruit.

Potato Salad with Homemade Grapefruit Mayo

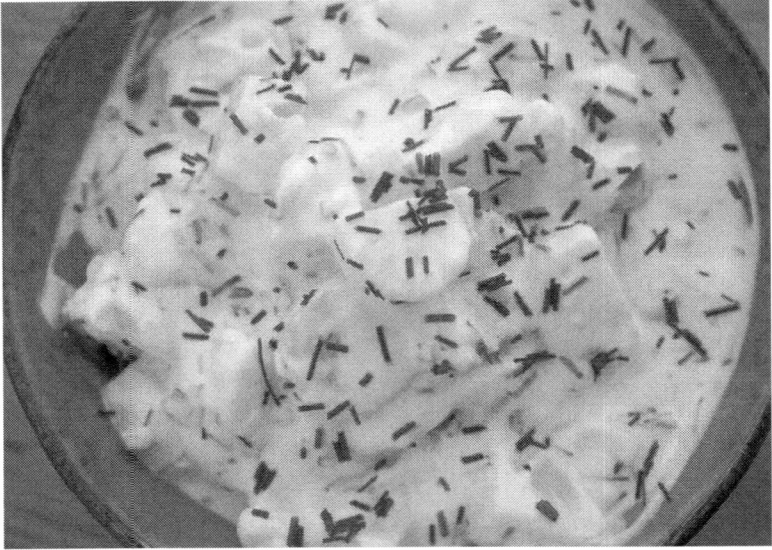

A creamy potato salad with a citrus mayo is ideal to serve with seafood or cold cuts of meat.

Servings: 6-8

Total Time: 1hour 55mins

Ingredients:

Mayo:

- ¾ cup liquid egg substitute
- ⅓ cup grapefruit juice (divided)
- 1 tsp sugar
- ½ tsp salt
- ¼ tsp dry mustard
- ¾ -1 cup canola oil
- 1 tsp fresh grapefruit zest

Potato Salad:

- 2 pounds red potatoes (washed, cut into bite-size chunks)
- ¾ cup freshly squeezed grapefruit juice
- 1 tbsp salt
- 1 red grapefruit (peeled, seeded, chopped)
- 2 hard-boiled, eggs (shelled, chopped)
- ¾ cup celery (sliced)
- 2 tbsp green onions (sliced)
- 2 tbsp fresh parsley (minced)
- ¼ tsp salt

Directions:

1. For the mayo: Combine the egg substitute with the half of the grapefruit juice, sugar, salt and mustard to a food blender and process to combine.

2. Set the blender to high speed and gradually pour half of the canola oil in a thin stream into the blender. You can do this by pouring it through the opening in the top of the blender jug by the lid.

3. Add the remaining juice to the blender, again in a fine stream, followed by the remaining canola oil, again in a fine stream. The amount of oil will depend on your desired consistency.

4. Process until thickened and smooth.

5. Stir in the grapefruit zest and transfer to the fridge in a container that is covered for 60 minutes.

6. For the salad: Add the potatoes, grapefruit juice, and salt to a 4-quart capacity pan. Pour in sufficient water to cover the potatoes.

7. Over high heat, bring to boil before reducing to moderate heat and cooking for 10 minutes, until the potatoes are fork tender.

8. Drain the potatoes and place them in a bowl.

9. Add the mayo to the bowl and toss to coat evenly.

10. Add the pieces of grapefruit along with the eggs, celery, green onions, parsley, and seasoning. Stir gently until incorporated.

11. Cover with a lid an entirely chill before servings.

Red Snapper and Grapefruit Ceviche

This ceviche the ideal appetizer for any fish-loving family members or friends. What's more, it's buffer-friendly too.

Servings: 4

Total Time: 40mins

Ingredients:

- 10 ounces red snapper
- ¼ cup of freshly squeezed lime juice
- ¼ cup freshly squeezed grapefruit juice
- 2 Roma tomatoes (chopped)
- ½ grapefruit (seeded, cut into sections)
- 3 large garlic cloves (peeled, diced)
- ½ red onion (peeled, chopped)
- 1 jalapeno (finely chopped)
- ¼ cup cilantro (chopped)
- 1 just ripe avocado (peeled, pitted, chopped)
- Salt and black pepper
- Cracker, tortillas, chips (to serve, optional)

Directions:

1. Add the snapper to a bowl. Pour the lime and grapefruit juice over the fish.

2. Transfer to the fridge for approximately 25 minutes, or until the fish is white throughout.

3. Drain the juice from the red snapper and discard.

4. Transfer the fish to a clean bowl and add the tomatoes, grapefruit, garlic, red onion, jalapeno, cilantro, and avocado.

5. Season Serve with crackers, tortillas or chips.

Scallops with Grapefruit and Bacon

Juicy scallops, zesty grapefruit, and salty bacon are a winning trio of flavors and make for a flavor-packed appetizer.

Servings: 4

Total Time: 35mins

Ingredients:

- 1 large grapefruit
- 3 ounces bacon (cut into 1x ¼ "matchsticks)
- Salt and black pepper
- 20 sea scallops
- ¼ cup onion (peeled, minced)
- ½ cup Sauvignon Blanc
- 2 tbsp capers (drained)
- 2 tbsp unsalted butter

Directions:

1. Peel the grapefruit and remove the pith.

2. Over a bowl, with a knife, release the fruit by cutting in between the membranes. Over a second smaller bowl, squeeze the juice to yield 3 tablespoons.

3. In a frying pan, over medium heat, cook the bacon for 3 minutes, until crispy.

4. Using a slotted spoon transfer the bacon to a plate, and pour off all the bacon fat apart from 1 tbsp.

5. Season the sea scallops and all them to the pan, cooking over moderate heat, for 3 minutes, until browned.

6. Flip the scallops over and add the onion, cooking over medium heat until the scallops are just cooked through, for an additional few minutes. Transfer to a plate.

7. Pour in the wine along with the grapefruit juice to the pan and over medium heat, bring to simmer. Cook while scraping up the brown bits in the pan.

8. Strain the liquid into heat safe cup, before returning it to the pan.

9. Add the capers along with the butter and cook, while shaking the frying pan, until the sauce thickens, for 2-3 minutes.

10. Add the scallops along with any juices to the pan, turning them to coat with the sauce evenly.

11. Stir in the grapefruit together with the bacon and serve.

Shrimp Salad with Grapefruit and Mint

Enjoy this healthy seafood and fruit salad to enjoy as an appetizer.

Servings: 4

Total Time: 40mins

Ingredients:

- 2 tbsp freshly squeezed lime juice
- 2 tbsp freshly squeezed grapefruit juice
- 1 tsp soy sauce
- 1 tbsp fish sauce
- 1 tsp sriracha sauce
- 1 tsp sugar
- ⅛ tsp salt
- ⅓ cup thinly sliced shallots (thinly sliced)
- 1 tbsp peanut oil
- 1 pink grapefruit
- ½ pound cooked pink shrimp (peeled)
- ¼ cup carrot (grated, refrigerated)
- ¼ cup cilantro (chopped)
- 1 avocado (peeled, pitted, medium diced)
- 4 servings butter lettuce leaves (washed, dried, torn into bite-size pieces)
- ¼ cup dry-roasted salted peanuts (roughly chopped, to garnish)
- ¼ cup fresh mint leaves (cut into thin ribbons, to garnish)

Directions:

1. Using a small jar with re-sealable lid, prepare the marinade. Combine the lime juice with the grapefruit juice, soy sauce, fish sauce, sriracha sauce, sugar and salt and transfer to the fridge.

2. Sauté the shallots in the peanut oil over moderate to high heat for 10 minutes, until caramelized. Allow to cool before setting to one side.

3. Peel the grapefruit, remove and discard the pith and slicing horizontally cut into ½" rounds. Next, slice into ½" wide strips, before cutting into medium-sized cubes. Lightly salt and transfer to the fridge.

4. Rinse and pat the shrimp, dry.

5. Add the shrimp to a bowl followed by the carrots, cilantro, avocado, and shallots.

6. Add the marinade to the bowl and toss to combine evenly.

7. Allow the shrimp to marinate for 20 minutes in the fridge.

8. Tear the leaves into bite-size pieces and portion out into 4 individual bowls.

9. Spoon the cubes of grapefruit over the top and add the shrimp mixture on the top, and drizzle with a drop of excess marinade.

10. Garnish with chopped peanuts along with the mint and serve.

Sweet 'n' Sour Meatballs with Grapefruit

Your guests will love these pork meatballs in a citrus sauce which can either be made half their size and served on cocktail sticks or larger size with rice.

Servings: 4

Total Time: 1hour 10mins

Ingredients:

- 2 cloves garlic (peeled, minced)
- 1 medium egg
- 1 tbsp soy sauce
- 1 tbsp cornstarch
- 1 tsp ground ginger
- ½ tsp Chinese 5-spice powder
- 1 pound ground pork
- ½ cup onions (peeled, finely diced)
- 1 tbsp vegetable oil

Sauce:

- 1 cup granulated sugar
- ⅓ cup cornstarch
- 2 cups Florida grapefruit juice
- ⅓ cup white vinegar
- 2 tbsp soy sauce
- 2 tsp ground ginger
- 1 red pepper (seeded, cut into ½" pieces)
- 2 Florida grapefruit

Directions:

1. In a bowl, whisk the garlic with the egg, soy sauce, cornstarch, ginger, and Chinese 5-spice.

2. Add the ground pork and onion, mixing to combine.

3. Divide the meatballs into 16 equal portions and using clean hands, form each portion into a 1½" diameter ball shape.

4. Over moderate to high heat, heat the oil in a large frying pan or skillet.

5. In batches, add the meatballs to the pan and brown all over. Drain away any fat and set to one side.

6. In the meantime, in a large pan, whisk the sugar with the cornstarch.

7. Pour in the grapefruit juice along with the vinegar, soy sauce, and ginger.

8. Cook while occasionally stirring, over moderate heat, until the mixture begins to thicken and boil.

9. Add the cooked meatballs to the sauce.

10. Turn the heat down to low, cover and continue to cook, simmering for 35 minutes.

11. Fold in the red pepper, cover and cook for an additional 5 minutes.

12. In the meantime, cut the rind from the grapefruit along with pith and using knife cut sections away from the membrane. Add to the sauce and allow to heat through for 60 seconds.

13. Serve and enjoy.

Sweet Potatoes with Grapefruit

Regular mash flavored with orange is a regular dish in Europe but sweet potatoes combined with grapefruit takes this side dish to a whole new taste level.

Servings: 4

Total Time: 1hour 25mins

Ingredients:

- 1¾ pounds sweet potatoes
- 1 large grapefruit
- 3 tbsp unsalted butter
- ⅓ cup firmly packed light brown sugar
- ¼ tsp salt
- 2 medium eggs (well beaten)

Directions:

1. Preheat the main oven to 375 degrees F.

2. Unpeeled, add the potatoes to a large pan and pour in sufficient water, to cover.

3. Using a swivel-blade veggie peeler, peel the zest from the grapefruit and add it to the potatoes.

4. Bring boil before reducing the heat to a simmer, and simmer for 20 minutes, until the potatoes are fork tender.

5. In the meantime, using kitchen tongs, dip the grapefruit into the boiling water and blanch, while occasionally turning for 30 seconds.

6. Briefly rinse the grapefruit under cold running water to cool and remove the pith.

7. Over a bowl, section the grapefruit and peel off the membranes. Set the juice and pulp to one side and discard the pips.

8. Once the potatoes are tender, drain, discard the zest and set aside to cool.

9. Peel the potatoes and transfer to a food processor together with the pulp, juice, butter, brown sugar and salt. Process to a puree consistency.

10. Add the eggs, mixing to combine.

11. Transfer the sweet potato mixture to a well-buttered, 6-cup soufflé dish.

12. Place in a pan of hot water and bake until the center is set, for 45 minutes.

Zucchini Spaghetti with Grapefruit and Brazil Nuts

A healthy alternative to regular pasta, these zucchini spaghetti-like ribbons are perfectly combined with lots of herbs, nuts and zesty segments of grapefruit.

Servings: 4

Total Time: 12mins

Ingredients:

- 2 large zucchini
- 1 cup brazil nuts
- ¼ tsp sea salt
- 3 tbsp water
- ½ cup basil
- ½ cup coriander
- 2 tbsp olive oil
- Freshly squeezed juice of ½ lemon
- 1 small garlic clove (peeled, minced)
- 2 grapefruits (peeled, seeded, segmented)

Directions:

1. Using a mandolin or spiralizer, cut the zucchini into spaghetti-like ribbons and set to one side.

2. In a food blender, combine the brazil nuts with the sea salt, water, basil, coriander, oil, lemon juice, and garlic. Process to a pesto-like consistency, adding additional water, if needed.

3. Fold the pesto into the zucchini noodles and garnish with segments of grapefruit.

4. Serve.

Mains

Asian Lamb and Grapefruit Noodle Salad with Ginger Dressing

When the weekend arrives why reach for the takeout menu when this healthy and tasty Asian dish can be prepared in no time at all!

Servings: 6

Total Time: 35mins

Ingredients:

- Sunflower oil
- 3 banana shallots (thinly sliced)
- Salt and black pepper
- 3 (5 ounce) lamb leg steaks (trimmed of fat)
- 2 pink grapefruits
- 1 cucumber (peeled into ribbons, seeded)
- 1 red chili (thinly sliced)
- Small bunch of mint (leaves picked)
- 7 ounces rice noodles (cooked)

Ginger Dressing:

- 1 thumb-sized piece ginger (peeled, finely grated)
- 2 tbsp soy sauce
- 2 tbsp rice wine vinegar
- 1 tbsp soft brown sugar
- 2 tsp toasted sesame oil

Directions:

1. Fill a pan with sufficient oil to fill halfway and heat.

2. When the oil is hot enough that a shallot when dropped in the oil, sizzles with 30 seconds fry the shallots until golden brown.

3. Using a slotted spoon, remove the shallots from the oil and allow to drain on kitchen paper towel. Season and set to one side.

4. Heat a large skillet until hot.

5. Rub the lamb all over with a drop of oil and season.

6. Cook the lamb for between 2-3 minutes on each side for medium, timings will depend on the thickness of the lamb.

7. Transfer to a platter and loosely tent with aluminum foil. Set aside to rest for between 5-10 minutes.

8. In the meantime, using a fruit knife, remove the peel from the grapefruits.

9. Over a bowl and to catch the juices, cut the fruit into segments. Add the segments to the bowl along with the ginger, soy sauce, rice wine vinegar, soft brown sugar, and toasted sesame oil, stir to combine.

10. Add the cucumber along with the chili, mint and noodles and any lamb juices. Toss to fully combine, making sure that the ingredients are evenly coated before transferring to a platter.

11. Cut the lamb into thin slices and arrange on top of the salad.

12. Garnish with shallots and serve.

Beef with Tangy Grapefruit Chimichurri Sauce

The perfect dish for a special occasion; juicy steak in a flavorsome chimichurri sauce.

Servings: 6-8

Total Time: 1hour 45mins

Ingredients:

- 4 garlic cloves (peeled)
- 3 cup fresh parsley (coarsely chopped)
- 3 cups fresh cilantro (chopped)
- 2 tbsp fresh oregano leaves (chopped)
- 1 tsp red pepper flakes
- Salt and black pepper
- 1 cup freshly squeezed grapefruit juice
- 2 tbsp extra-virgin olive oil
- 2 pounds flank steak

Directions:

1. Add the garlic, parsley, cilantro, oregano, red pepper flakes, salt and pepper to a food processor, cover and on the pulse setting process until finely chopped.

2. In a fine stream, add the grapefruit juice along with the oil while the processor runs and blend until silky smooth allow to stand for an hour.

3. In the meantime, season the steak and over moderate heat, grill to your preferred level of doneness.

4. Remove from the heat and allow the steak to rest for several minutes.

5. Diagonally and across the grain, slice the flank steak.

6. Serve with the sauce and enjoy.

Citrus-Molasses Glazed Ham

Everyone loves a glazed ham but instead of the usual orange-honey glaze why not instead include freshly squeezed grapefruit to the glaze.

Servings: 12

Total Time: 2hours 20mins

Ingredients:

- 1 (7-9 pound) cooked bone-in ham

Glaze:

- ½ cup freshly squeezed grapefruit juice
- ½ cup freshly squeezed orange juice
- ¼ cup molasses
- 3 tbsp honey
- 1 tbsp packed brown sugar
- 1 tbsp Dijon mustard
- 3 tsp coarsely ground pepper

Directions:

1. Preheat the main oven to 325 degrees F.

2. Arrange the ham on the baking rack in a shallow roasting tin.

3. With a sharp knife, score the ham with ¼" deep cuts in a diamond-shape pattern.

4. Cover and bake the ham until it reaches an internal thermometer registers 130 degrees F for between 1¾-2¼ hours.

5. In the meantime, in a pan, combine the grapefruit with the orange juices and bring to boil, cooking for between 6-8 minutes, or until the liquid is reduced by 50 percent.

6. Stir in the remaining ingredients (molasses, honey, brown sugar, mustard, and pepper) and bring to boil. Turn the heat down and uncovered, simmer for between 12-15 minutes, until the mixture thickens.

7. Take the ham out of the oven and brush with 1/3 cup of the glaze.

8. Bake in the oven, uncovered, while occasionally basting with any remaining glaze, until the ham registers an internal temperature of 140 degrees F, this will take an additional 15-20 minutes.

Creamy Gnocchi with Grilled Asparagus and Grapefruit

Give gnocchi a zesty citrus makeover with grilled grapefruit.

Servings: 4

Total Time: 20mins

Ingredients:

- 1 pound asparagus (ends trimmed)
- 1 large ripe pink grapefruit (cut into 8 wedges)
- 1 tbsp olive oil
- Salt
- 1 tbsp butter
- 1 tbsp flour
- ¼ cup heavy cream
- 1 cup chicken stock
- 1 pound potato gnocchi
- Salt and black pepper
- Chives (to garnish)

Directions:

1. Over high heat, bring a large pan of salted water to boil. Preheat your grill to high.

2. Place a skillet over moderate heat.

3. In a bowl, toss the asparagus with the grapefruit and oil and season with salt.

4. Add the butter along with the flour to the skillet, whisking to combine.

5. Sauté the roux for between 1-2 minutes, until golden.

6. Whisk in the cream followed by the chicken stock and allow the sauce to simmer and thicken before turning off the heat.

7. In the meantime, drop the gnocchi into the boiling water and cook according to the package directions.

8. Ladle the gnocchi into the cream sauce while setting the pasta cooking water aside. Toss to coat evenly.

9. Grill the asparagus and the grapefruit for 2-3 minutes on each side, until char marks begin to form.

10. Cut the asparagus into 1-1½ segments and toss into the pasta. You may need to add a drop of pasta cooking water to thin.

11. Serve each bowl of gnocchi with 1-2 wedges of grilled grapefruit, garnish with chives and enjoy.

Grapefruit Rubbed Short Ribs

Enjoy tender rib meat that literally melts off the bone cooked in a grapefruit marinade. Serve with a fresh green salad.

Servings: 2

Total Time: 2hours 45mins

Ingredients:

Rub:

- 1 cup dark brown sugar
- 1 tbsp smoked paprika
- 2 tsp ground ginger
- ¼ tsp cayenne pepper
- ½ tsp ground coriander seeds
- 2 tsp garlic powder
- 2 tsp freshly ground black pepper
- Pinch of salt
- Zest of ½ grapefruit

Ribs:

- 2 pounds braising beef short ribs
- ½ cup water
- Freshly squeezed juice of ½ grapefruit

Directions:

1. Preheat the main oven to 325 degrees F.

2. In a bowl, stir the brown sugar with the paprika, ginger, cayenne, coriander, garlic, pepper, salt, and grapefruit zest.

3. Liberally coat the ribs in the rub and place in a 9x13" roasting tin.

4. Pour the remaining sugar over the top of the ribs, patting down to create a thick layer.

5. In a small bowl, combine the water with the grapefruit juice and pour the mixture into the bottom of the roasting tin.

6. Cover the roasting tin with aluminum foil and cook in the oven for 90 minutes.

7. Remove the aluminum foil and continue roasting for an additional 60 minutes.

8. Remove and discard the liquid from the tin and enjoy.

Pork Tenderloin in a Curry Grapefruit Marinade

Grapefruit is such a versatile fruit, from pies to pork it a go-to kitchen staple.

Servings: 4

Total Time: 2hours 25mins

Ingredients:

- 4 dried chipotle chiles (stemmed, seeded)
- 1 tbsp garam masala
- 1 cinnamon stick
- ½ cup fresh ruby red grapefruit juice
- 1 tbsp honey
- 1 tbsp sugar
- 1 tsp cider vinegar
- 1 tsp kosher salt
- 1 pound pork tenderloin (fat trimmed)
- 1 tsp vegetable oil

Directions:

1. In a coffee mill or grinder, grind the chipotles, garam masala, and cinnamon to a powder-like consistency.

2. Using a non-reactive, large baking dish, combine the ground spices with the grapefruit juice, honey, sugar, cider vinegar, salt and 1 tbsp of water, stirring to dissolve the salt and sugar entirely.

3. Add the pork tenderloin and turn to coat with the marinade evenly.

4. Transfer to the fridge for 2 hours, while occasionally stirring.

5. Light your grill and using a damp kitchen paper towel, carefully coat the grill with oil.

6. Over a moderate to hot fire, grill the pork, turning until sufficiently cooked through for approximately 15 minutes.

7. Transfer to a chopping board and allow to stand for 5 minutes.

8. In a non-reactive small pan, over medium-high heat, boil the marinade, for 4 minutes, until reduced to a glaze.

9. Slice the meat into ¼" thick slices and serve with the glaze.

Roasted Duck Breasts with Grapefruit Sauce

Serve these roasted duck breast slathered with grapefruit sauce and a side order of sweet potato pancakes.

Servings: 4

Total Time: 45mins

Ingredients:

- 2 tbsp honey (divided)
- 1 tsp sugar (divided)
- ⅔ cup freshly squeezed grapefruit juice (divided)
- 4 (6 ounce) duck breast halves (scored in a criss-cross pattern)
- 1 cup chicken stock
- ¼ cup heavy cream
- 2 fresh thyme sprigs
- 1 tbsp unsalted butter
- 1 grapefruit (peeled, seeded, segmented)
- Salt and black pepper
- Sweet potato pancakes (store-bought)

Directions:

1. Preheat the main oven to 350 degrees F.

2. In a bowl, combine a ¼ teaspoon of honey, ¼ teaspoon of sugar and 2 tablespoons of grapefruit juice. Brush the mixture all over the duck.

3. Heat a large oven-safe frying pan or skillet.

4. When the pan is sufficiently hot, add the duck breasts, skin side facing downwards and over low heat, sear for 5-6 minutes, until browned.

5. Flip the breast over and cook for a couple of minutes, before roasting in the oven for 5 minutes.

6. Allow the duck to rest on a chopping board for 4 minutes, while loosely tenting with aluminum foil.

7. In the meantime, in a non-reactive small pan, mix the remaining sugar with 1¼ teaspoons of honey and 1 tablespoon of duck fat from the pan.

8. Cook until the mixture is light brown before adding the stock, cream, thyme and the remaining grapefruit juice.

9. Over medium heat, simmer until reduced to ½ cup.

10. Stir in the butter and grapefruit segments and season.

11. Remove the pan from the heat.

12. Thinly slice the duck and place on warm plates along with the pancakes.

13. Spoon the grapefruit sauce over the top and serve.

Seared Cod with Grapefruit Slaw

A simple main course to serve with a delicious cabbage slaw is ideal for any time of year.

Servings: 4

Total Time: 35mins

Ingredients:

- ½ head savoy cabbage (cut into quarters, cored, shredded)
- ½ red onion (peeled, thinly sliced)
- ¼ cup parsley (chopped)
- 2 tbsp freshly squeezed lemon juice
- ¼ cup extra-virgin olive oil (divided)
- Salt and black pepper
- 2 grapefruits (seeded, segmented)
- 4 (6 ounce) skinless, boneless cod fillets (patted dry)

Directions:

1. Combine the shredded cabbage with the red onion and chopped parsley.

2. Drizzle with lemon juice along with 2 tbsp oil and toss to coat. Season.

3. Transfer to the fridge for a minimum of 20 minutes. Toss with the segments of grapefruit just before you are ready to serve.

4. In a pan, heat the remaining oil over moderate to high heat.

5. Season the fish, add to the pan cook while turning over once until golden for 7-9 minutes.

6. Serve with the homemade slaw.

Spanish-Style Citrus Paella

Serve this paella with a crusty baguette and enjoy with family and friends as an ideal weekend treat. Ole!

Servings: 6-8

Total Time: 1hour

Ingredients:

- 5 tbsp olive oil (divided)
- 1 medium yellow onion (peeled, minced)
- 1 green bell pepper (chopped)
- 1 cup tomato (seeded, chopped)
- 1 tbsp garlic (peeled, minced)
- 1 tsp ground cumin
- 1 tsp dried basil (crumbled)
- 1 tsp dried thyme (crumbled)
- 1 bay leaf
- 2 pounds boneless, skinless chicken breasts (cut into strips)
- 4 Spanish chorizo links (cut into slices)
- 3½ cups chicken broth
- 1 cup freshly squeezed grapefruit juice
- ¼ tsp saffron
- 3 cups long-grain rice
- 1 pound mussels (scrubbed, beards removed, rinsed)
- 1 pound raw large shrimp (peeled, deveined)
- 1 cup fresh peas
- Cilantro (minced, to garnish)
- Grapefruit wedges (to garnish)

Directions:

1. In a frying pan, heat 3 tbsp of oil and add the onion along with the bell pepper and cook until softened, for 2 minutes.

2. Add the tomato followed by the garlic, cumin, basil, thyme and bay leaf and cook until the majority of the liquid has evaporated, for 5 minutes. Set to one side.

3. In a frying pan, heat 2 tbsp of oil over medium-high heat until hot.

4. Add the chicken breasts and sear for between 1-2 minutes, until gently browned.

5. Transfer the chicken strip to a plate and put aside.

6. Add the chorizo and while stirring, cook until lightly browned on both sides.

7. Using a slotted spoon, remove the chorizo from the pan and add to the chicken strips on the plate.

8. Preheat the main oven to 400 degrees F.

9. In a pan, bring the chicken broth, grapefruit juice, and saffron to simmer.

10. Add the rice to a 14" paella suitable pan or oven-safe skillet.

11. Arrange the chicken mixture on top.

12. Arrange the mussels along with the shrimp on top.

13. Pour in the simmering chicken broth-saffron mixture.

14. Bake the paella in the oven for half an hour without stirring. You may need to add additional chicken broth if the mixture is too dry.

15. Add the peas and bake the paella until the mussels are open, and the liquid is absorbed, for approximately 10 minutes.

16. Cover the paella with a clean tea towel and allow to stand for 5 minutes.

17. Garnish with cilantro and wedges of grapefruit.

Spicy Citrus Po' Boy with Grapefruit Slaw

A tasty shrimp Po'Boy gets an upbeat makeover with homemade grapefruit slaw.

Servings: 2

Total Time: 40mins

Ingredients:

Slaw:

- 1 grapefruit (peeled, segmented, chopped)
- 1 cup daikon radish (grated)
- 1 carrot (peeled, grated)
- ¼ cup cilantro (chopped)
- Salt and pepper
- Freshly squeezed juice of ½ lime

Batter:

- 1 cup panko breadcrumbs
- ½ cup flour
- 1 tbsp cornstarch
- 2 tsp garlic powder
- 1 tsp onion powder
- ½ tsp cayenne pepper
- 1 tsp chili powder
- ¼ cup soda water
- 1 medium egg

Additional Ingredients:

- 2 cups vegetable oil
- 3 tbsp mayonnaise
- 2 tsp garlic chili sauce
- 8 medium raw tiger shrimp (washed, peeled, deveined)
- 2 dill pickles (sliced)
- 2 fresh sausage buns
- Lime wedges (to serve)

Directions:

1. In a bowl, combine the grapefruit with the radish, carrot, cilantro, seasoning and fresh lime juice.

2. Add the breadcrumbs to a small shallow dish and put to one side.

3. In a second small bowl, combine the mayonnaise with the chili sauce and put to one side.

4. In a pan, heat the oil to 375 degrees F.

5. For the batter: In a bowl, whisk the flour with the cornstarch, garlic powder, onion powder, cayenne pepper, chili powder, soda water, and egg. Whisk until combined.

6. In batches, dip the shrimp in the batter followed by the breadcrumbs.

7. Fry the shrimp until golden for between 4-6 minutes.

8. Remove the shrimp from the pan and transfer to a kitchen paper towel lined plate.

9. Spread the inside of each of the buns with chili mayo, and top with the homemade slaw, cooked shrimp and pickles.

10. Serve with lime wedges and enjoy.

Desserts

Baked Grapefruit Alaska

A baked Alaska is lot easier than you may think and this dessert with fresh grapefruit is great dessert to serve during National Grapefruit Month.

Servings: 4

Total Time: 30mins

Ingredients:

- Segments of 2 grapefruits (membranes removed, plus any juices)
- 6 tbsp granulated sugar
- Whites of 4 large eggs
- 4 generous scoops of good-quality vanilla ice cream

Directions:

1. Preheat the main oven to 425 degrees F.

2. Transfer the grapefruit segments and reserved juices to a bowl along with 2 tbsp sugar.

3. Divide the fruit between four individual ramekins.

4. Whisk the egg whites until they can hold stiff peaks. Add the remaining 4 tbsp sugar and continue to whisk until stiff.

5. Place one scoop of ice cream in each ramekin on top of the grapefruit and spread over the egg white so that the perimeter of the ramekin is sealed.

6. Arrange on a cookie sheet and bake for 8-9 minutes until the meringue is crisp.

7. Serve straight away.

Caramelized Grapefruit Bread Pudding

Liven up this homey, and traditionally heavy, dessert with zesty grapefruit.

Servings: 8

Total Time: 1hour 50mins

Ingredients:

- 2½ tbsp salted butter (at room temperature)
- 15 thin slices French bread
- ⅓ cup raisins
- 1 cup grapefruit juice
- 2 cups whole milk
- ⅓ cup + 2 tbsp brown sugar
- 4 medium eggs (beaten)
- ½ tsp grapefruit zest
- 1 tsp cinnamon
- Segments of 2 grapefruits (membranes removed)

Directions:

1. Preheat your oven to 350 degrees F.

2. Butter each slice of bread on one side. And arrange in a shallow baking dish, butter-side down. Scatter over the raisins.

3. In a bowl, whisk together the grapefruit juice, milk, 2 cups sugar, eggs, zest, and cinnamon until combined.

4. Pour the mixture over the bread and set aside for half an hour.

5. Arrange the baking dish in a roasting tin and pour hot water into the roasting tin, ¾ of the way up the sides of the baking dish.

6. Bake in the oven for approximately 50-55 minutes until set in the center.

7. Take out of the oven and preheat your broiler.

8. Arrange the grapefruit segments on top of the pudding and sprinkle over the 2 tbsp sugar. Place under the broiler until the sugar melts and caramelizes on top.

9. Serve warm.

Champagne Sorbet with Mango and Grapefruit

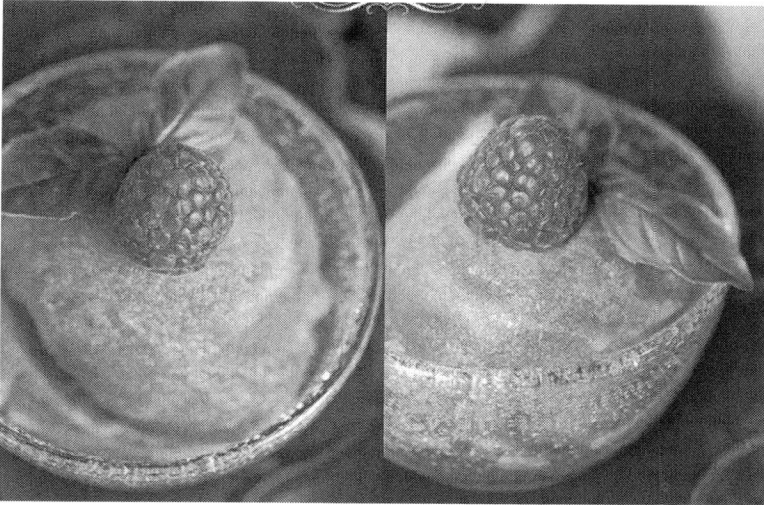

This sophisticated palette cleansing sorbet is ideal for any celebration thanks to a generous glug of champagne.

Servings: 6-8

Total Time: 6hours 30mins

Ingredients:

- 1 cup grapefruit juice
- 1½ cups mango puree
- 1 cup champagne
- ⅓ granulated sugar
- Fresh mint

Directions:

1. Combine the grapefruit juice, mango puree, champagne, and sugar in a saucepan over moderate heat and bring to a boil. Take off the heat and chill until ice-cold.

2. Transfer the mixture to an ice cream churner and process using manufacturer instructions. Transfer to a resealable container and freeze until firm.

3. Garnish with mint before serving.

Cherry-Citrus Cobbler

This zesty cobbler will soon become a new family favorite, thanks to its bold fruity flavor.

Servings: 8

Total Time: 1hour

Ingredients:

Filling:

- ½ cup fresh orange juice
- 4 cups pitted cherries
- 1 tbsp fresh lemon juice
- 1½ cups granulated sugar
- 3 tbsp cornstarch
- 2 tbsp butter
- 2 cups orange segments (membranes removed)
- ½ cup pink grapefruit segments (membranes removed)

Topping:

- 6 tbsp brown sugar
- 1 cup all-purpose flour
- ½ tsp cinnamon
- 1 tsp baking powder
- 3 tbsp unsalted butter
- 3 tbsp whole milk
- 1 large egg (beaten)

Directions:

1. Preheat the main oven to 350 degrees F.

2. In a bowl, combine orange juice, cherries, lemon juice, sugar, and cornstarch. Transfer to a saucepan and place over moderate heat, bring to a simmer while continually stirring for 60 seconds. Take off the heat.

3. Stir in the butter until it melts, followed by the orange and pink grapefruit segments.

4. Transfer the mixture to a baking dish.

5. Next, prepare the topping.

6. Add the sugar, flour, cinnamon, and baking powder to a food processor. Pulse to combine, then add the butter and pulse again until the mixture is crumbly.

7. Transfer to a mixing bowl along with the milk and the egg and stir until only just combined.

8. Drop the mixture roughly on top of the filling. Place in the oven and bake for approximately half an hour until golden and bubbly.

9. Allow to cool to warm before serving.

Chewy Grapefruit Macaroons

These soft and chewy French coconut cookies get a delicious citrus makeover.

Servings: 30

Total Time: 35mins

Ingredients:

- ⅔ cup granulated sugar
- Whites of 4 eggs
- 3 tbsp fresh grapefruit juice
- 1 tsp vanilla essence
- ¼ tsp salt
- 3 tsp grapefruit zest
- ½ cup all-purpose flour
- 4½ cups shredded coconut
- Melted white chocolate (optional)

Directions:

1. Preheat the main oven to 325 degrees F. Cover a cookie sheet with parchment.

2. Whisk together the sugar, egg whites, grapefruit juice, vanilla essence, and salt until combined. Stir in the zest.

3. In a second bowl, combine the flour and coconut. Fold the dry ingredients into the wet until combined.

4. Roll the mixture into 2" balls and arrange on the baking sheet. Bake for just over 10 minutes until golden. Allow to cool.

5. Dip each cool macaroon halfway into melted white chocolate to coat the base. Allow to set before serving.

Coconut and Grapefruit Shaved Ice

This refreshing shaved ice will go down a treat with the kids, and grownups too!

Servings: 6-8

Total Time: 4hours 15mins

Ingredients:

- 8 ounces fresh-squeezed grapefruit juice
- 3 cups canned green coconut water
- ⅓ cup granulated sugar

Directions:

1. Stir together the grapefruit juice, coconut water, and sugar until the sugar dissolves.

2. Pour the mixture into a rimmed baking tin and freeze overnight.

3. When ready to serve, use a fork to rake the ice until snow-like.

Fluffy Marshmallow and Grapefruit Mousse

Marshmallow crème brings an irresistible cloud-like fluffiness to this citrus mousse.

Servings: 6

Total Time: 8hours 10mins

Ingredients:

- 6 tbsp granulated sugar
- Juice of 1 grapefruit
- 2 (4") pieces grapefruit peel
- Yolks of 2 large eggs
- 1 cup marshmallow crème
- 1 cup heavy cream

Directions:

1. Add the sugar, grapefruit juice, and 2 of the peel strips to a saucepan over moderate heat and bring to a boil while continually stirring. Heat for several minutes until the sugar dissolves, and the mixture is thick and syrupy. Take off the heat.

2. In a bowl, whisk the egg yolks. Pour half of the syrupy grapefruit juice into the yolks slowly. Whisk to combine, then pour the egg/grapefruit syrup mixture back into the pan.

3. Place over low heat and gently warm for a few minutes until thickened.

4. Strain into a bowl set inside a large bowl of ice to cool quickly.

5. In a room temperature bowl, stir the marshmallow cream until smooth then pour in the grapefruit custard and fold until incorporated.

6. Next, whip up the cream until stiff, then fold into the mousse mixture.

7. Divide between serving cups and chill for a few hours before serving.

Gingersnap Pie with Grapefruit Curd

A velvety smooth grapefruit curd sits inside a golden brown gingersnap crust. The ultimate combination!

Servings: 4

Total Time: 9hours 30mins

Ingredients:

Crust:

- 1⅛ cups gingersnap cookie crumbs
- 3 tbsp brown sugar
- 1 cup walnuts
- 4 tbsp melted butter

Filling:

- 4 tbsp cornstarch
- 1 cup granulated sugar
- Yolks of 4 eggs
- Pinch salt
- ¼ cup fresh-squeezed lemon juice
- 1½ cups fresh-squeezed red/pink grapefruit juice
- 5 tbsp butter (chopped)

Directions:

1. Preheat the main oven to 350 degrees F.

2. Add the cookie crumbs, sugar, and walnuts to a food processor and blitz until combined. Add the melted butter and pulse until combined.

3. Transfer the mixture to a 9" pie tin and press into the base and sides.

4. Place in the oven and bake for just over 10 minutes until golden. Allow to cool.

5. Whisk together the cornstarch, sugar, egg yolks, and salt in a saucepan until combined. Next, whisk in the fresh-squeezed juices.

6. Place the pan over moderate heat and bring to a boil for 60 seconds while stirring continually. Take off the heat.

7. Immediately whisk in the pieces of butter until glossy and thick.

8. Strain the curd into the pie crust and allow to cool. Chill overnight before serving.

Glazed Grapefruit and Yogurt Cake

This moist and fluffy glazed sponge is perfect served alongside a hot cup of afternoon tea or coffee.

Servings: 12

Total Time: 1hour 35mins

Ingredients:

Cake:

- 2 tsp baking powder
- 1½ cups all-purpose flour
- ¼ tsp salt
- 1 cup plain yogurt
- 3 eggs
- ⅓ cup granulated sugar
- ¼ cup honey
- 5 tbsp grapefruit zest
- ¼ cup canola oil
- ½ tsp vanilla essence

Glaze:

- 2½ tsp grapefruit juice
- ½ cup powdered sugar
- Grapefruit (cut into wheels)
- Fresh mint

Directions:

1. Preheat the main oven to 350 degrees F.

2. Combine the baking powder, flour, and salt in a bowl.

3. In a second bowl, whisk together the yogurt, eggs, sugar, honey, grapefruit zest, oil, and vanilla essence.

4. Fold the dry mixture into the wet mixture until incorporated and transfer to a 9" springform tin. Place in the oven and bake for just under half an hour until golden. Allow to cool.

5. In the meantime, prepare the glaze.

6. Stir together the grapefruit juice and powdered sugar until smooth and drizzle-able.

7. Pour the glaze over the cooled cake and garnish with fresh grapefruit wheels and mint.

Grapefruit Creamsicle Sorbet

Forget orange, grapefruit creamsicle will soon become your new favorite flavor, especially when brought to life as a zesty and refreshing sorbet.

Servings: 8

Total Time: 6hours 35mins

Ingredients:

- 1-quart vanilla ice cream (softened)
- 1¼ cups water
- 1¼ cups white sugar
- 2 tsp dried hibiscus
- 1 tbsp grapefruit zest (grated)
- 1½ cups fresh-squeezed grapefruit juice

Directions:

1. Transfer the ice cream to one half of a standard loaf tin leaving the other side free for later. Cover and freeze for 1½ hours.

2. In a pot over moderate heat, combine the water and sugar and bring to the boil until the sugar dissolves. Take off the heat, stir in the hibiscus and zest, and set aside for 10 minutes.

3. Strain the mixture, discard solids, and stir in the grapefruit juice. Cover and chill for 1½ hours.

4. Transfer the chilled grapefruit/hibiscus mixture to an ice cream churner and process according to manufacturer directions.

5. Scoop the mixture into the empty half of the loaf tin. Cover and freeze for a few hours until firm.

Greek Yogurt and Grapefruit Brulee

This delicious dessert is a healthy take on the calorific French classic, crème brulee. Now you can indulge your sweet tooth guilt free!

Servings: 4

Total Time: 15mins

Ingredients:

- Segments of 2 ruby red grapefruit (membranes removed)
- ¼ cup brown sugar
- ½ cup vanilla-flavor Greek yogurt

Directions:

1. Preheat your oven's broiler.

2. Divide the grapefruit between 4 oven-proof dishes and sprinkle over the sugar.

3. Place under the broiler until the sugar is melting.

4. Serve straight away alongside a dollop of vanilla yogurt.

No-Churn Ruby Red Grapefruit Gelato

Great news, you don't even need an ice cream churner to make this to-die-for gelato.

Servings: 12

Total Time: 8hours 10mins

Ingredients:

- 1 cup granulated sugar
- 2 tbsp ruby red grapefruit zest
- 2 cups whipping cream
- ¼ cup fresh ruby red grapefruit juice
- Pinch salt

Directions:

1. Whisk together the sugar, zest, cream, juice, and salt until combined. Pour the mixture into a 9" square dish and freeze overnight until firm.

Vanilla Rice Pudding with Pink Grapefruit

Thick and creamy rice pudding with a comforting vanilla aroma is balanced with vibrant pink grapefruit.

Servings: 4

Total Time: 1hour

Ingredients:

- 1 cup long grain white rice
- 5 cups whole milk
- 1 cinnamon stick
- ½ cup white sugar
- Scrapings of 1 vanilla bean
- 1½ pounds pink grapefruit (peeled, separated into segments, membranes removed)
- Yolks of 2 large eggs
- ¼ tsp salt

Directions:

1. Bring a medium-sized pot of water to a boil. Stir in the rice and cook for several minutes then drain.

2. In a second saucepan, stir together the milk, cinnamon, sugar, vanilla bean scrapings, and rice, Place over moderately high heat and bring to a simmer. Stir often to prevent sticking. Turn the heat down low and cook for approximately half an hour until thick and creamy.

3. Take off the heat. Remove the cinnamon stick and stir in the egg yolks until incorporated. Allow to cool a little.

4. Divide between bowls, top with grapefruit and serve,

Vanilla-Grapefruit Cheesecake

This melt-in-the-mouth dessert with smooth vanilla and bittersweet grapefruit is guaranteed to satisfy any cheesecake lover.

Servings: 12

Total Time: 9hours 30mins

Ingredients:

- 2 cups graham cracker crumbs
- 1 cup + 3 tbsp granulated sugar
- 5 tbsp melted butter
- ½ cup sour cream
- 1½ pounds cream cheese (at room temperature)
- 1 tsp grapefruit zest
- ¼ cup grapefruit juice
- 4 medium eggs
- 1 tsp vanilla essence
- Segments of 1 grapefruit (membranes removed)
- 1 tsp crystallized ginger (diced)

Directions:

1. Preheat the main oven to 325 degrees F.

2. Bring a medium-sized pot of water to a boil.

3. Wrap the base and sides of a 10" springform tin with plastic wrap then foil.

4. In a bowl, combine the cracker crumbs, 3 tbsp sugar, and melted butter. Press the mixture into the base of the tin. Set to one side.

5. In a second bowl, beat together the sour cream, cream cheese, grapefruit zest, and juice until fluffy.

6. Beat in the eggs one at a time, then stir in the vanilla essence. Spoon the mixture over the crust.

7. Arrange the tin in a larger roasting tin and pour the boiling water into the roasting tin, so it reaches halfway up the sides of the springform.

8. Place in the oven and bake for just over an hour until set.

9. Allow to cool before chilling overnight.

10. Garnish with ginger before serving.

White Chocolate Grapefruit Brownies

Homemade grapefruit jam gives these decadent white chocolate brownies an addictive fruity tang.

Servings: 18

Total Time: 1hours 35mins

Ingredients:

- Butter (to grease)

Brownies:

- 3 ounces white chocolate chunks
- 7 tbsp salted butter
- 1 cup white sugar
- Pinch salt
- 3 tbsp fresh grapefruit juice
- Zest of 1 grapefruit
- 2 medium eggs
- ¾ cup all-purpose flour

Jam:

- Scrapings of ½ a vanilla pod
- Fruit and juice of 2 grapefruits (membranes removed)
- ½ cup brown sugar

Directions:

1. Preheat the main oven to 350 degrees F. Grease an 8" square tin and line with parchment.

2. In a saucepan, melt together the white chocolate and butter over low heat.

3. Add the sugar and salt to a bowl and stir in the melted chocolate.

4. Fold in the grapefruit juice and zest.

5. Beat in the eggs until combined. Next, fold in the flour.

6. Pour the batter into the baking tin and bake for just over 20 minutes. Allow to cool.

7. In the meantime, prepare the jam. In a saucepan over moderate heat, bring to a simmer the vanilla pod, grapefruit juice, fruit, and sugar. Stir well and cook for 20 minutes until thick and jammy. Take off the heat and allow to cool completely.

8. Spread the jam over the cooled brownies. Slice and enjoy.

About the Author

Martha Stone is a chef and also cookbook writer. She was born and raised in Idaho where she spent most of her life growing up. Growing up in the country taught her how to appreciate and also use fresh ingredients in her cooking. This love for using the freshest ingredients turned into a passion for cooking. Martha loves to teach others how to cook and she loves every aspect of cooking from preparing the dish to smelling it cooking and sharing it with friends.

Martha eventually moved to California and met the love of her life. She settled down and has two children. She is a stay at home mom and involves her children in her cooking as much as possible. Martha decided to start writing cookbooks so that she could share her love for food and cooking with everyone else.

THANK you VERY much !

Dear Reader,

Thank you very much for choosing my book. I hope you really enjoy it. If don't mind I would like to ask you to leave a review after reading.

Thanks.

Sincerely yours,

Stephanie Sharp

Made in the USA
Monee, IL
22 February 2020